Insects Around the World

All About North American Honey Bees

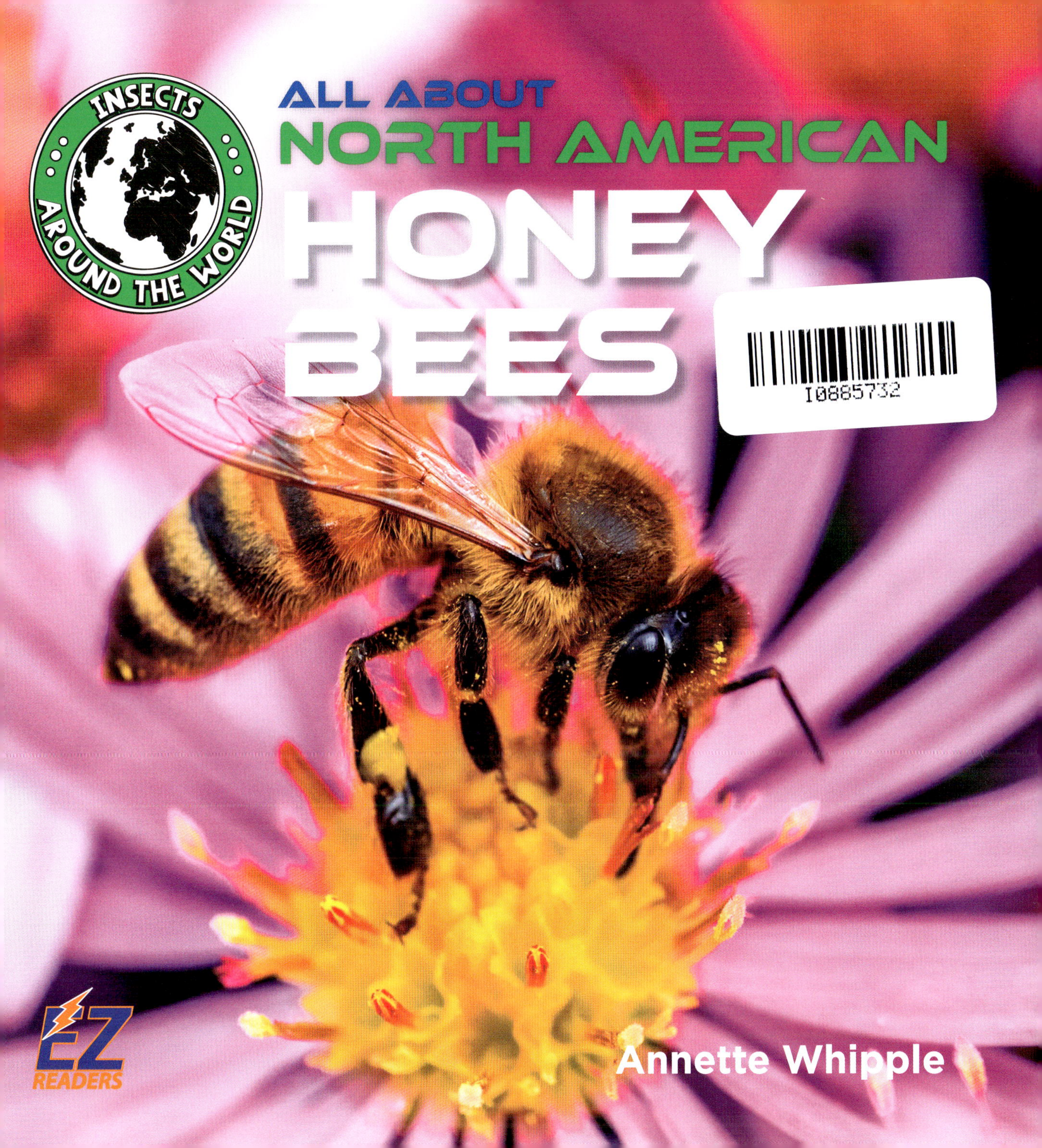

Annette Whipple

EZ Readers

Creating Young Nonfiction Readers

EZ Readers lets children delve into nonfiction at beginning reading levels. Young readers are introduced to new concepts, facts, ideas, and vocabulary.

Tips for Reading Nonfiction with Beginning Readers

Talk about Nonfiction

Begin by explaining that nonfiction books give us information that is true. The book will be organized around a specific topic or idea, and we may learn new facts through reading.

Look at the Parts

Most nonfiction books have helpful features. Our *EZ Readers* include color photographs and graphic aids, a table of contents, a glossary, and an index. Share the purpose of these features with your reader.

Color Photos and Graphic Aids

A lot of information can be found by "reading" photos, charts, maps, and other graphic aids found within nonfiction texts. Help your reader learn more about the different ways information can be displayed.

Table of Contents

Located at the front of the book, this list shows the big ideas within the text and the page numbers where they can be found.

Glossary

Located at the back of the book, the glossary defines key words and phrases that are related to the topic. These words and phrases can be found in the text in colored type.

Index

Located at the back of the book, an index is an alphabetical list of topics and the page numbers where they can be found.

With a little help and guidance about reading nonfiction, you can feel good about introducing a young reader to the world of *EZ Readers* nonfiction books.

Mitchell Lane
PUBLISHERS

2001 SW 31st Avenue
Hallandale, FL 33009
www.mitchelllane.com

First Edition, 2025.

Author: Annette Whipple
Designer: Rhea Magaro
Editor: Kim Thompson

Names/credits:
Title: All About North American Honey Bees / by Annette Whipple
Description: Hallandale, FL :
Mitchell Lane Publishers, [2025]

Series: Insects Around the World
Library bound ISBN: 978-1-68020-953-2
eBook ISBN: 978-1-68020-962-4

EZ Readers is an imprint of
Mitchell Lane Publishers

PHOTO CREDITS
Shutterstock: Jennifer Bosvert, cover, 1; Donamen, 4-5; MERCURY studio, 6-7; Megan Kobe, 8-9; Smeerjewegproducties, 10-11; MakroBetz, 12-13; Lehrer, 14-15; Yuliya Evstratenko, 16-17; Diyana Dimitrova, 18-19; wirakorn deelert, 20-21; nblx, 22; JoannaTkaczuk, 22; 135pixels, 22; Lois GoBe, 22

Paperback ISBN: 979-8-89260-141-2

CONTENTS

Honey Bees 4
Where Do Honey Bees Live? 22
Interesting Facts 23
Parts of a Honey Bee 23
Glossary 24
Index 24
Further Reading 24
On the Internet 24

Insects called honey bees have stripes. They have two big eyes and three smaller eyes. Tiny hairs cover their bodies. They're approximately the size of a dime. Honey bees weigh as much as a pinch of salt.

Honey bees have four wings. Their wings move so fast that they buzz. Their two **antennae** smell, taste, and touch the air.

Honey bees build hives from **beeswax**. More than 50,000 honey bees can live in a hive. The bee group is called a **colony**.

All bees have jobs. Some bees visit flowers to find food. They sip sweet **nectar** to take back to the hive. Then, it's made into honey. The bees also collect flower dust called **pollen**. They put it in pouches on their legs. Young bees eat pollen.

More bees want to find food. So, the bees tell others where to find flowers. They don't talk. They dance! The waggle dance tells the others where to find the food.

There are more jobs too. Some honey bees clean the hive. Others care for newly hatched eggs called **larvae**. Male **drones** mate with the queen. Some bees feed and clean the queen. The queen's job is to lay eggs. She lays about 1,000 eggs every day.

Honey bees also protect the queen and the colony. They sting predators when scared.

Honey bees huddle inside the hive in the winter. They buzz their wings to keep warm. They eat the honey they made during the summer.

People eat the bees' extra honey and use beeswax. Honey bees help people in another way too. They spread pollen so that plants can make seeds for new flowers. In this way, honey bees help make about one-third of the plants that people eat. We need honey bees.

WHERE DO HONEY BEES LIVE?

There are more kinds of bees in North America than in any other place in the world. Honey bees are just one species out of more than 20,000.

Honey bees live close to flowers. You can find honey bees in these habitats.

INTERESTING FACTS

- Honey bees store nectar in a special stomach called a crop.
- Honey bees steal honey from other hives.
- Honey bees live in hollow trees when human-built hives are not available.
- Honey bees die if they sting you.

PARTS OF A HONEY BEE

Antennae
Antennae are so important that honey bees have a special notch in their knees to use for cleaning their antennae.

Crop
A special organ called a crop holds nectar until the honey bee returns to the hive.

Eyes
The three little eyes of a honey bee help it to fly, and the two big eyes have thousands of lenses to help it see.

Pollen Basket
Hairs on the honey bee's hind legs make a pouch called a pollen basket.

Stinger
The barbed stinger gets stuck in skin while the honey bee flies away to die.

GLOSSARY

antennae (an-TEN-ee)
Feelers on the head of an insect

beeswax (BEEZ-waks)
A soft yellow material produced by glands in a bee's body

colony (KAH-luh-nee)
A large group of animals living together

drones (drohnz)
Male honey bees

insects (IN-sekts)
Small animals with hard outer skeletons, six legs, and three body sections

larvae (LAHR-vee)
Young insects after they hatch; the stage of life between an egg and a pupa when an insect looks like a worm

nectar (NEK-tur)
A sweet liquid made by flowers

pollen (PAH-luhn)
Powder made by flowers to help them reproduce

INDEX

colony 9, 17
food 11, 13
hive(s) 9, 11, 15, 18, 23
honey 11, 18, 20, 23
jobs 11, 15
nectar 11, 23
pollen 11, 20, 23
size 4

FURTHER READING

Fleming, Candace. *Honeybee: The Busy Life of Apis Mellifera*. New York, NY: Neal Porter Books, 2020.

van Frankenhuyzen, Robbyn Smith. *H Is for Honey Bee: A Beekeeping Alphabet*. Ann Arbor, MI: Sleeping Bear Press, 2020.

ON THE INTERNET

10 Facts About Honey Bees!
https://www.natgeokids.com/au/discover/animals/insects/honey-bees
Learn 10 buzzy facts about honey bees.

Honeybee
https://kids.nationalgeographic.com/animals/invertebrates/facts/honeybee
Learn even more about honey bees.